Peter Eldin

The Secret Agent's Handbook

with drawings by Roger Smith

BEWARE of Impostors!

secrets

An Armada Original

The Secret Agent's Handbook
was first published in 1977 in Armada
by Fontana Paperbacks,
14 St. James's Place, London SW1A 1PS

This impression 1981

© Peter Eldin 1977

Printed in Great Britain by
Love & Malcomson Ltd.,
Brighton Road, Redhill, Surrey

The Secret Agent's Handbook

Other titles by Peter Eldin in Armada

The Trickster's Handbook
The Whizzkid's Handbook
The Explorer's Handbook
Top of the Pops Quiz
Isn't That Amazing!

Coming soon!

The Millionaire's Handbook

Also in Armada

Crazy—But True!
More Crazy—But True!
The Armada Book of Jokes and Riddles
1st, 2nd & 3rd Armada Books of Fun
1st, 2nd & 3rd Armada Books of Cartoons
Jokes and Riddles from A–Z
The Awful Joke Book
The Armada Funny Story Book
Big Daddy's Joke Book

About the Author..

The name PETER ELDIN is an alias. The author's real name has been classified as secret by the official censor.

Peter Eldin was born in ████████████ ████████████████ where he still lives. He always eats ██████████ for his tea and usually goes to ██████ for his holidays.

This handbook consists of dossiers used in the training of Armada agents. The information it contains is confidential — do not divulge it to anyone who has not been cleared by security. To give you an indication of the amount of secrecy surrounding the information given in these files the dossiers have been classified as follows:

Unrestricted contains information which is of value to all Armada agents but which is known generally.

Secret contains material that may also be in the hands of the enemy agents but which should still be kept secret just in case the enemy are not aware of it.

Top Secret should not be divulged under any circumstances.

✳ ✳ ✳ *Armada Agents Only.* This information is dynamite! It is known only to Armada agents of the highest calibre—guard it with your life.

Important..

This book contains top secret information.
It must not fall into the hands of the enemy.
If you are captured by enemy agents and this hand-
book is in your possession — swallow it.

Contents..

DOSSIER.. SAH/OO1
SUBJECT.. Agents' Headquarters
CLASSIFICATION.. Unrestricted

Although the successful agent will spend a lot of his time away on special missions he will also need a base from which to operate. This can take many forms and will depend upon the agent's particular needs and what facilities are available.

A bedroom in a house can be used as effective headquarters as enemy agents will not suspect that such an innocent place would be used as a base for secret activities. Security devices can be fixed to the doors, windows, and cupboards to ensure that all secret information in the room is kept secure. Details of some security devices are given in other dossiers in this handbook.

A notice board (see dossier SAH/017) can be put on the wall to convey information to other agents.

An old shed or garage can be similarly adapted to the needs of a group of secret agents. To make the HQ more pleasant, the inside can be painted by the agents in the group, but be sure that you get the owner's permission before doing so. The owner should, of course, be cleared by security before he is told the purpose of the building.

If a room or shed are not available for your HQ how about building one of your own? Interested agents should refer to dossier SAH/010 for futher information.

DOSSIER.. *SAH/002*
SUBJECT.. *Torn Towns*
CLASSIFICATION.. *Unrestricted*

All agents know that they should destroy secret information as soon as they have read it. Secret Agent 008 (he is one up on his brother James) Premium Bond received a list of cities in which he had to carry out assignments. Unfortunately he tore it up before he had memorised it. The torn pieces are pictured here. Can you put them together to find out where Premium Bond has to go?

The answer can be found on page 126.

Agents must be able to react quickly in an emergency. Their reflexes must be sharp. This device has been devised so that you can test the reaction times of the agents in your group.

All you need is a strip of paper measuring about five centimetres by twenty centimetres. Draw five divisions on the strip and mark each section as shown on the blueprint included with this dossier.

To use the reaction tester, hold it in one hand and have the agent to be tested put his finger and thumb on either side of the paper at the bottom. He must not be touching the paper. You now drop the paper through his fingers and he must try to catch it by closing his finger and thumb. He is, of course, not allowed to do this until you have let go.

Take a look at the section where he has caught the paper and then assess his suitability as an agent from the following list.

If he catches it in section five he is either a top agent, or he has cheated.

Section four — excellent reaction and will make a good agent for the group.

Section three — very good. This man will make a good, steady agent but he should not be given too much responsibility.

Section two — average reaction which signifies an average and reliable agent.

Section one — his reflexes are too slow to be effective on assignment. Use him for routine tasks only.

If he missed the paper altogether he is too slow to become an agent. Suggest that he practices to improve his reaction speed.

Secret agents, like many other specialist groups, use many words that are understood only by others in the same occupation. Here are some words that all agents should know:

Black operations Blackmailing, discrediting, or even killing an enemy agent.

Bug A miniature radio receiver or microphone used to listen-in to what is happening in a particular room.

A BUG.

CARELESS TALK

Cannon A pickpocket who works for an agent.

Contact Someone that an agent has to meet for a particular purpose. Often a *password* is used so that the agent can identify his contact.

Courier Someone who carries secret messages, documents, or information.

Dirtying The process of restoring a room to normal after it has been searched or *bugged*. This means that the room must not be cleaner than it was before so that all the dust, and even the cobwebs must be replaced!

17

Drop   A place where secret messages are left.

Fix   To get someone accused of a crime of which he is innocent.

Letter box   Someone who holds secret messages awaiting collection by an agent.

Master spy   The head of a *spy ring*.

Measles   If someone has "got the measles" it means that he is dead.

I'm afraid you're dead.

Peep   An agent who specialises in secret photography and the use of *pins*.

Pin   Photographic lens that is so small it can be hidden in ordinary objects without being spotted.

Set-up   A trap to catch an unsuspecting agent.

Shadow   Someone who follows another person secretly.

Sneakie   Another name for a *bug*.

Spy ring   A group of spies or secret agents.

Sugar   A bribe.

Tail   Another name for a *shadow*.

Wireman   An agent who specialises in electronic listening devices such as bug and sneakies.

DOSSIER.. SAH/005
SUBJECT.. *It's a Fact*
CLASSIFICATION.. *Unrestricted*

An Egyptian agent in the days of the Pharaohs had a secret message tattooed on his head. In order to deliver the message he had to have his hair cut.

During the siege of Paris in the Franco-German War of 1870–1 priests were allowed to walk out of the city and wander through the German lines. The Germans did not realise that they were French agents in disguise.

Mata Hari is one of the best known women spies of all time. She was also one of the most inefficient and made up the legends that surround her name.

One of the first textbooks ever written included a large section on the art of the secret agent. It was called "The Art of War" by Sun Tzu and was published in China 2,500 years ago.

Mary Queen of Scots had some secret letters sent to her in waterproof bags hidden in kegs of beer.

During the First World War windmills were used in France and Belgium to send secret messages.

Christine Granville, a secret agent in the Second World War, was once arrested after smuggling four pilots across the Yugoslav border. She persuaded her German captors that she was simply having a picnic and made them restart her car which had stalled.

What agents always stay in bed?
Undercover agents

Why do Soviet agents work fast?
Because they are always rush'n

What disease is known as "secret service flu"?
A code in the head

What do agents in an atomic plant eat?
Nuclear fission chips

What British agent lies in a pond and croaks?
Bullfrog Drummond

When do agents work in shops?
When they are working on counter-espionage

What sort of spy is delicious to eat?
A min spy

What sort of agent does everything twice?
A double agent

What is black, has six legs, wears a disguise, and listens to people?
A secret bug

Which famous spy was red, tasty, and delicious in a salad?
Tomata Hari

When is a spy well mannered?
When he's a-gent

DOSSIER.. SAH/007
SUBJECT.. Spy Traps
CLASSIFICATION.. Secret

One of the things that you will want to know while you are away on special missions is whether or not anyone enters your headquarters during your absence. Here are some methods of finding out if anyone has been tampering with your secret equipment.

Tie a thin thread across all the doorways about twenty centimetres from the ground. If, when you return, you find the thread broken, you will know that someone has entered your hideout.

Use saliva to stick a hair across the opening of a drawer. When someone opens the drawer the hair will drop off and reveal to you that your files have been tampered with. Hairs can also be stuck to windows in case someone tries to get in that way.

Another method of detecting whether or not papers have been tampered with is to position a small bead on the top sheet of a pile of papers. If anyone moves the pile the bead will roll off and you will know that the papers have been disturbed.

If you have a pile of papers on your desk run a pencil line down the edge of the pile. If the pile is disturbed when you are away, the pencil line will be uneven when you return.

Open some drawers slightly and then place a pencil mark on the side, or underneath, of the drawer to mark its position. Even someone who opens and closes the drawer extremely carefully will not be able to position it exactly on the pencil mark if they do not know of its existence.

Sharpen all your pencils to the finest point you can manage before you leave your headquarters. By examining the pencil points when you return from your mission you will soon know whether or not anyone has been using them.

Another way is to actually provide the enemy agent with something to write on. Get a sheet of carbon paper and place it about two sheets down in a notepad. Leave the notepad open on your desk while you are away. If someone uses the pad to copy any of your confidential records you will know exactly what they have taken. All you have to do is open the pad at the sheet beneath the carbon paper. There you will find a perfect impression of anything that was written on the top sheet of the pad during your absence.

Keep all your equipment, files, and other belongings neat and tidy. In this way you will soon notice if they have been disturbed. Keeping things tidy also has the added advantage that you can easily find anything when you want it.

DOSSIER.. SAH/008
SUBJECT.. Vowel Language
CLASSIFICATION.. Secret

This is a simple code that you and your fellow spies will find easy to learn and remember. Because it is so simple it is also easy to decipher and should therefore be used only in situations where it is not possible to make use of any of the other codes described in this handbook.

All you need to know are the five vowels in alphabetical order:

A E I O U

When you write your message, all you do is change the vowels in each word for the next vowel in sequence. For A you use E, for E you use I, for I use O, for O use U, and for U you use A. It is as simple as that.

Here is a practice message for you to decode: "Errovong et fruntoir et modnoght. Meki sari thet thi gaerds eri dostrectid su O cen git ecruss thi burdir ansiin. Buros."

If you read it correctly it said:
"Arriving at frontier at midnight. Make sure that the guards are distracted so I can get across the border unseen. Boris."

If enemy agents should discover that you are using this code, you can simply arrange with your own agents to change the order of the vowels from time to time so that instead of using AEIOU you utilise IEAUO or some other sequence. That should put the enemy off the scent.

A similar method of coding messages will be found in dossier SAH/025.

Buy some record cards, or postcards, from your local stationer and write on each the headings: name, address, age and description. You will also need an ordinary ink pad (also from the stationer) or some thick paint. You are now equipped to record the fingerprints of the agents in your group.

Other details about this agent, such as his code name, missions accomplished, and so on can also go on this card.

Keep the cards in a strong box and make sure that it does not get taken by the enemy or all of your men will be placed in danger.

If an enemy agent infiltrates your organisation posing as one of your contacts you have only to check your card index file and compare his thumbprint with that on the card to find out that he is false.

This fingerprinting and card record can also be made to keep a dossier on any enemy agents that you may capture.

DOSSIER.. SAH/010
SUBJECT.. Branch Headquarters
CLASSIFICATION.. Unrestricted

If a room or a shed cannot be commandeered for use as your group's headquarters (see dossier SAH/001) it is possible to build suitable premises. You may be able to do so in a tree, but if you do plan this type of headquarters they must be absolutely safe. A senior agent will have to be called in to supervise construction. The tree you choose must have branches tough enough to take the weight of the building with people inside it, and the planks that form the floor of your headquarters must be good strong ones, firmly fixed to the branches so they are as level as possible.

Having built a solid floor, it is a fairly simple matter, using more planks, to build a tree hut that will make a fine headquarters. The entrance to the hut can be either through the floor or through one of the sides. A length of thick rope tied to one of the branches will provide the way of getting up and down. If enemy agents are in the vicinity the rope can be pulled up out of the way so that you are safe from attack.

SECURITY NOTE: During secret meetings at any of the hideouts described in dossiers SAH/001 and 010 it would be as well to post a guard outside to make sure that no-one tries to listen to your confidential plans.

Remember the old wartime adage: "Walls have ears."

To prevent anyone getting too close without your knowledge the camp could be surrounded with alarms like the ones described in dossiers SAH/021 and 055.

DOSSIER.. SAH/011
SUBJECT.. Group Symbol
CLASSIFICATION.. Unrestricted

This dossier gives instructions for making a block for printing your group's symbol on notepaper and official documents. All you need is a potato and an ink pad, or some thick paint.

Cut the potato in half and then carve a symbol on to the cut face of the potato. The symbol must be cut in reverse to make it come out the right way when it is printed.

Now all you have to do is to press the cut symbol on to the ink pad, or paint, and then transfer it to the notepaper, record card, or special pass that you are printing.

DOSSIER.. SAH/012
SUBJECT.. Shopping List Code
CLASSIFICATION.. Top Secret

This code is known to only a few selected agents. Keep it a secret and do not divulge it to an enemy agent under any circumstances.

To most people this message will look just like a simple shopping list but the prices give you a clue as to its real purpose. If you look at each price and then count that number of letters from the beginning of that item you will arrive at a letter. When you have done the same for every item in the list you will be able to read the message. Thus the first item is *ham 2p*. The price tells you that the important letter is the second one, A. In the next item bread, the price is 1p so you take the first letter, B. Can you now read the rest of the message?

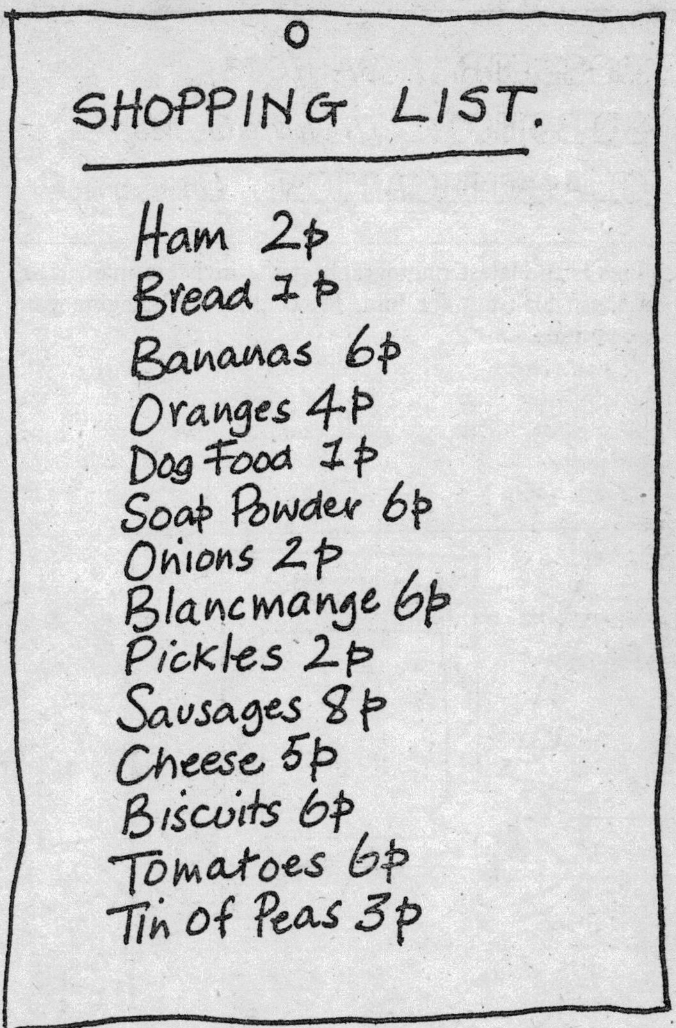

SHOPPING LIST.

Ham 2p
Bread 7p
Bananas 6p
Oranges 4p
Dog Food 7p
Soap Powder 6p
Onions 2p
Blancmange 6p
Pickles 2p
Sausages 8p
Cheese 5p
Biscuits 6p
Tomatoes 6p
Tin of Peas 3p

You will find the answer on page 126.

When you have done this see if you can make up some shopping lists to send messages to your friends.

B

DOSSIER.. SAH/013
SUBJECT.. *The Invisible Man*
CLASSIFICATION.. *Unrestricted*

This is the latest photograph of the invisible man. Keep a sharp look out for him. He could be sabotaging your operations.

DOSSIER.. SAH/014
SUBJECT.. *Direction Finding*
CLASSIFICATION.. *Secret*

If, during an assignment, you have to cross country and you do not have a compass, you can use your watch instead.

All you have to do is to follow the instructions detailed in this dossier:

First place your watch on the ground or on a flat rock.

Next turn it so that the hour hand points towards the sun.

Now that part of the watch that lies exactly on the mid-point of the shortest distance between the hour hand and the number twelve is pointing directly to the south (if the time is after six p.m. it will be pointing to the north).

This may sound rather complicated at first but it is really quite simple. Let us take an example to see how it works in practice.

We will assume that it is three o'clock in the afternoon. First point the hour hand (on the three) towards the sun. Now the mid-point on the shortest distance between the three and the twelve is at seven and a half minutes past the hour. That point is the direction of south. This example is shown diagrammatically in the first of the illustrations included in this dossier. The other illustrations give some further examples to demonstrate how straightforward the procedure is.

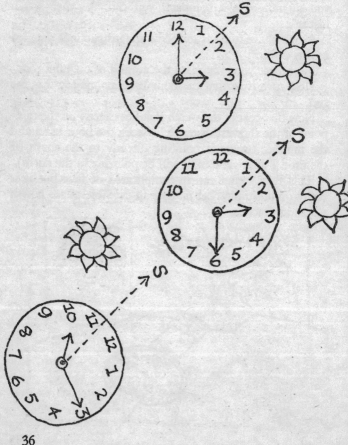

It is a good idea to give each agent in your group a special identity card. This should bear his name, a small photograph, and the group symbol (see dossier SAH/011). The top leading agent of the group should sign the identity card to prevent forgeries.

At each meeting of the group all agents should show their cards before the session starts. This will help prevent enemy agents from getting into your secret briefing sessions.

DOSSIER.. SAH/016

SUBJECT.. Matchstick Men Messages

CLASSIFICATION.. Unrestricted

A simple method of writing secret messages is to use matchstick men in place of letters of the alphabet. The alphabet shown in this file can be used but, for security reasons, agents are advised to work out their own system in collaboration with their fellow agents.

The message at the bottom of the page uses the code shown below. Can you work out what it says?

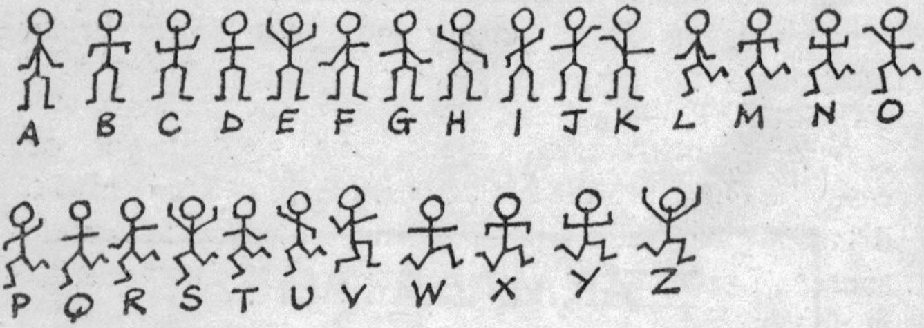

You will find the answer on page 126.

DOSSIER.. SAH/017
SUBJECT.. Agents' Notice Board
CLASSIFICATION.. Unrestricted

A simple notice board for your headquarters can be made quite easily with a few polystyrene ceiling tiles. These tiles come in a variety of sizes so the number you will need will depend upon the size of tile that you use and how big you want your notice board to be.

The tiles can simply be stuck to the wall. If you cannot stick them on the wall, glue them on to a backing sheet of cardboard and then hang it up. Be careful to select the correct glue or you may burn the tiles. Ask at the shop where you buy the tiles for the correct type of glue to use.

Notices, instructions, maps, and photographs can easily be pinned to the notice board with ordinary pins or drawing pins. Such a notice board will provide a useful source of information and communication for the agents in your group.

DOSSIER.. SAH/018
SUBJECT.. *Ground to Air Signals*
CLASSIFICATION.. *Unrestricted*

When aeroplanes crash and there is no means of radio communication with rescue planes, pilots use the international ground to air code of emergency signals to convey messages. The signals are drawn on the ground with large stones, sticks, white cloth, or anything else that can be seen clearly from the air. This code is known by pilots all over the world. Agents should learn the code for use in emergencies.

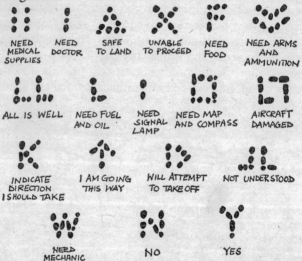

The code can also be used for passing messages to contacts by scratching the designs in the earth so that your colleagues will see it.

DOSSIER.. SAH/019
SUBJECT.. Secret Handshakes
CLASSIFICATION.. Secret

When working on an assignment it is essential that you should be able to recognise friendly agents. One way to do this is to invent some special handshakes that are known only to the members of your group. Some are given in this dossier but you should also try to devise some of your own.

A simple form of secret handshake is to just put your thumb into your palm as you extend your hand in greeting. If your colleague does the same you will know that he is on your side. You will not be able to clasp hands by this method, just put your hands together, but both of you will know that you are safe in the other's company.

invent
some
special
hand-
shakes

For handshake number two you grip the other person at the elbow and your contact does the same.

Grasp each other at the elbow

Another way to shake hands when meeting fellow agents is to do a normal handshake — but using the left hands. This form of greeting should not be used if you are working in enemy territory as it is fairly well known.

Try to devise special handshakes for your group. You could greet your colleague by placing your right hand on his left shoulder, or by turning the hand as you greet him.

Once you have decided on your special greeting be sure to keep it a secret. Enemy agents are always on the look-out for classified information that they can report back to their masters — so be on your guard at all times.

DOSSIER.. SAH/020
SUBJECT.. Figure It Out
CLASSIFICATION.. Unrestricted

The strange designs shown on this page were once part of a secret coded message. One design, however, is missing. Can you work out what the designs represent and what the missing design should look like?

The answer is on page 126.

DOSSIER.. SAH/021
SUBJECT.. *Burglar Alarm*
CLASSIFICATION.. *Unrestricted*

To prevent anyone creeping up on you when you are at work in your hideout, make this burglar alarm.

All you need is a length of thin cotton, a stick, and a sheet of tin. If a sheet of tin is not available a metal tray or the lid of a biscuit tin will work just as well.

Tie the cotton to a tree at waist height and then run it across the pathway that leads to your hideout. Tie the other end of the cotton to the stick and use the stick to support the sheet of metal.

As soon as someone walks along the path they will break the cotton. The stick will topple over and the sheet of tin will crash to the ground. Put some stones on the ground so that the tin makes a good clatter when it falls.

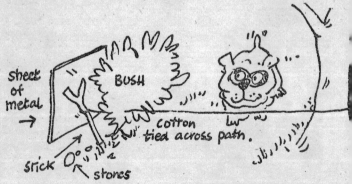

Put several of these alarms around your headquarters and you will know immediately when someone is approaching — and from which direction.

It is essential that agents should not flinch from their duty when carrying out assignments behind enemy lines. It may even be necessary at times for agents to operate in areas under enemy fire. To give new agents valuable combat experience, it is recommended that the training area be equipped with strategically placed cassette tape recorders. The tapes on the recorders should be of the sounds of gunfire, tanks, and other battle noises. If tape recorders are not available other agents in the group can make the appropriate noises.

During these simulated battle conditions the agent under training is required to tackle an assault course set out in the training area. Suitable items to be included in the assault course could be a heavy blanket under which the agent has to crawl, an obstacle to be jumped over, a sturdy rope strung from a tree to swing from one part of the course to the other, and so on. A time should be set for the course and agents will not be accepted as fully qualified until they can complete the course in the given time.

Using this method of battle simulation, training can be carried out in private gardens and other small areas and will provide all agents with useful experience of war-time conditions.

DOSSIER.. SAH/023
SUBJECT.. Secret Compass
CLASSIFICATION.. Secret

Get a magnet and a needle. Stroke the needle several times with the magnet. Always stroke in one direction, from the point towards the eye. When you have done this the needle will be magnetised. Pin it behind your lapel where, if it is discovered by an enemy agent, it will not be considered of any importance.

This magnetised needle will make a handy compass if ever you get stranded in a strange place. All you have to do is tie a length of thread to the centre of the needle and let it hang down. When it stops spinning the eye of the needle will be pointing to the north.

If you do not have any thread from which to hang the needle you can use it as a compass this way: Get a cup of water and float a piece of tissue paper or a small leaf on the surface. Place the needle on top of the leaf very carefully. Then push the leaf under the water and the needle will remain floating on the surface. It will then spin round so that the eye faces north. You can use this information to enable you to head for safety.

DOSSIER.. *SAH/024*
SUBJECT.. *It's in the Book*
CLASSIFICATION.. *Secret*

To use this code you and your contact must first agree upon a particular book that you will use. You must both have a copy of this book available for sending and receiving messages.

To send a message you look through the book for the first word of the message, then write down the page number on which the word appears, followed by the position that the selected word occupies on that page. Thus, if this was the book used, the word "copy" could be coded by the number 48.25 because the word "copy" is the twenty-fifth word on page 48.

This procedure has to be followed for every word in the message so that eventually the complete message would look something like this:

14.33   38.41   20.4   16.18   61.44

(This is not a real message)

When your contact receives the message he knows that the figures in front of each full stop represent a page number and the number after the full stop represents the particular word on that page.

For this code, you and your agents need first to agree on a keyword. This word should be changed from time to time just in case an enemy agent has infiltrated your organisation and discovered one of the keywords.

This is how the code is devised. First write down the keyword. (Let's use WIZARD for this example.) And then write down the rest of the alphabet, omitting the letters already used in the keyword.

W I Z A R D B C E F G H J K L M N O P Q S T U V X Y

Underneath this write the alphabet in its correct order:

W I Z A R D B C E F G H J K L M N O P Q S T U V X Y
A B C D E F G H I J K L M N O P Q R S T U V W X Y Z

Now write your message, referring to the table you have just made, substituting the letter above the one that you wish to use. So the word BEWARE would become I R U W O R, and so on.

See if you can read this message using the code word WIZARD: -

IRUWOR PLHAEROP WOR PRWOZCEKB
XLSO WORW

A better way to operate this code is not by using a word but a string of unrelated letters as the codeword. It works exactly the same way. If we were to use YMABFTW as the codeword, our table would look like this:

Y M A B F T W C D E G H I J K L N O P Q R S U V X Z
A B C D E F G H I J K L M N O P Q R S T U V W X Y Z

The advantage of this method is that your contact does not need to know the codeword in advance. When you send him a message, the first word that you use is the codeword itself, like this:

YMABFTW WFQ KRQ KT QCF YOFY NRDAE

He knows that the first word is the keyword and he uses that to decipher the rest of the message which reads:

GET OUT OF THE AREA QUICK

What does this message say?

ZPRCM SDOMM QTPIZOEJMQ OMLKOSMC EJ XKTO ZOMZ AEJC KTS SDMEO MWZRS LKQESEKJ ZJC OMLKOS PZRG

The answer is on page 126.

The initials on this page all have some connection with security or espionage around the world. Do you know what they mean?

The answers can be found on page 126.

DOSSIER.. SAH/027
SUBJECT.. Enemy Surveillance
CLASSIFICATION.. Secret

There will be times when you are on a special mission that you will have to keep suspects under observation. It is essential during such operations that you see without being seen. A good way of achieving this is to use a periscope. The instructions and blueprint comprising this dossier explain how you can make such a periscope for use on your assignments.

You will need a sheet of cardboard, glue, scissors, and two small mirrors of the same shape and size.

Draw the plan shown in this dossier on to the sheet of cardboard and cut it out. For security reasons, it is not possible to give any measurements for this piece of equipment. Armada agents will, however, be able to deduce that the blueprint is drawn to scale and that the size of the cardboard cut-out will in fact be determined by the size of the mirrors used. The letters on the blueprint indicate measurements that will all be of the same length.

Having cut out the cardboard, fold it along the dotted lines so that it forms a square tube. Open out the cardboard again and glue the mirrors into the positions marked x. Put glue on the shaded areas, form the cardboard back into a tube, and hold the apparatus firmly in position until the glue has set.

You now have a periscope that will prove invaluable on assignments. It can be used for looking over high walls, to keep subjects under observation, and it will also prove useful for looking around corners to check that the coast is clear before advancing.

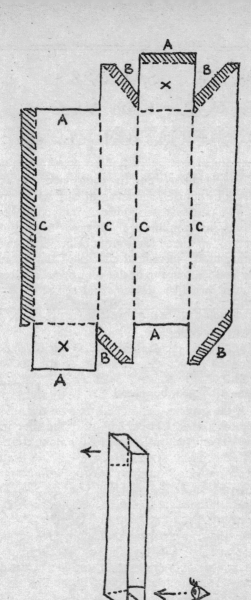

 EYE

53

DOSSIER.. SAH/028
SUBJECT.. Code Words
CLASSIFICATION.. Unrestricted

This is a simple but very effective code that can be worked out in detail by yourself and an agent with whom you are working on a particular assignment. First you make a list of sentences that you are likely to need in your under-cover work. A specimen list is given below. As each agent is operating under specialised conditions this is only an example. You will have to devise your own list according to your own particular problems and needs.

Watch out, you have been spotted

Meet me at *** o'clock

Abandon all operations immediately

Head for the border

This room is bugged, be careful what you say

For each sentence that you are likely to need you and your contact devise a list of alternative sentences similar to the following:

Watch out, you have been spotted
I think that it is going to rain

Meet me at *** o'clock
*There is a good show on the radio at
*** o'clock*

Abandon all operations immediately
Please cancel my newspapers

Head for the border
I hear you are going on holiday

This room is bugged, be careful what you say
You do not look very well

When you meet your contact you use the substitute phrase instead of the true sentence. If enemy agents are secretly listening to your conversation, they will not realise the true significance of what you have said. Because of this, any phrases that you make up must appear to be natural and part of your normal conversation.

As soon as you and your contacts have memorised a few alternative sentences, like those given above, you can then begin to add to the list so that you have alternative, and secret, sentences to cover almost every situation that may arise whilst you are on an assignment.

DOSSIER.. SAH/029
SUBJECT.. Wheels Within Wheels
CLASSIFICATION.. Top Secret

A useful method of devising codes for sending secret messages to another agent is the cipher wheel. This is how you and your fellow agents can make your own.

You will need a sheet of cardboard (an empty cereal packet is ideal), a pen or a pencil, and a paper fastener. (Stationers use the code name "bifurcated rivet" for this type of fastener.)

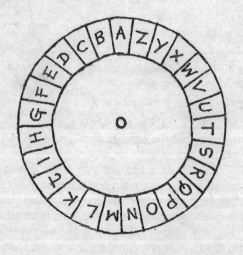

Trace the circles shown here on to the card and cut them out. Write the letters of the alphabet clockwise around the large circle and anti-clockwise around the small circle. Now place the small disc on top of the large disc and make a small hole through the centre of both of them. Push the paper fastener through the hole and bend the prongs out at the back so that the two discs are joined together but can still revolve.

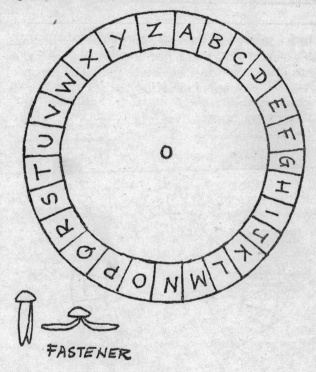

FASTENER

For instructions on how to use the cipher wheel, agents are advised to consult dossier SAH/031.

DOSSIER.. SAH/030
SUBJECT.. Toothpaste Hideout
CLASSIFICATION.. ✳ ✳ ✳

This is a useful way of keeping microfilms or other small items hidden without the risk of enemy agents finding them. Get an empty toothpaste tube and cut off the closed end. Rinse the tube out thoroughly.

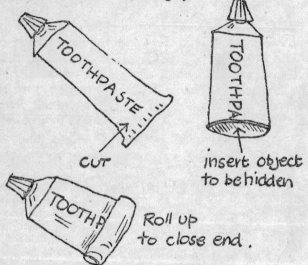

CUT

insert object
to be hidden

Roll up
to close end.

Put the top on the tube and insert the thing you wish to hide into the open end of the tube.

Now all you have to do is fold over the open end a couple of times so that it looks as if some of the toothpaste has been used. Keep the tube in your bathroom. No-one will think to look in an ordinary tube of toothpaste for such vital information.

To make use of a cipher wheel to transmit a secret message, follow these instructions:

Let us assume that the message you wish to send is:

MEET IN OLD CHURCH AT MIDNIGHT

First decide upon any letter of the alphabet. For this example we will use L. Now turn the inner disc of the wheel until the letter A is opposite your selected letter (L). Keep the wheels in that position while you write down the message. For each letter of the message you use the letter opposite it on the larger of the two wheels. Thus, instead of the letter A you will use L, and so on so that your completed message will look like this:

ZHHS DY XAI JERUJE LS ZDIYDFES

When you write out the secret message put the code letter (L) first so that your contact knows how to decipher it. To confuse the enemy it is as well to split the words into groups like this:

LZHHSD YXAI JER UJELSZ DIYD FES

When you are proficient at sending these codes you can increase the number of code letters you use to confuse enemy agents even further. Here is an example using a four-letter key:

First write down any four letters. For this example let us use WBRF.

This is your keyword. You use it to write the rest of the message as follows:

Turn the inner disc of the cipher wheel until the letter A is opposite the W (the first letter of the keyword) on the large wheel. Now look on the inner wheel for the first letter of the message, which in this case is T. You will find that it is opposite D. So D is the first letter of the coded message.

Now turn the inner disc until the A is next to the second letter of the keyword (B) and use that position to code the second letter (H) of the message. For the next letter you turn the inner wheel to R, and for the fourth turn it to F. You then start again at W and keep turning the discs to each subsequent letter of the keyword until you have coded the complete message.

You may find it easier if you first write out the message in one continuous line like this:

THESECRETFILESAREKEPTINTHEREDHOUSE

Then write the keyword, repeated several times, along the top of the message, like this:

WBRFWBRFWBRFWBRFWBRFWBRFWBRFWBRFWB
THESECRETFILESAREKEPTINTHEREDHOUSE

Now use the keyword to code the letters of the message as already explained and write the new letter underneath:

WBRFWBRFWBRFWBRFWBRFWBRFWBRFWBRFWB
THESECRETFILESAREKEPTINTHEREDHOUSE
DUNNSZABDWJUSJROSRNQDTEMPXABTUDLEX

Now, on another piece of paper, write down the keyword and follow it with the rest of the coded message split into five-letter groups, like this:

WBRFD UNNSZ ABDWJ USJRO
SRNQD TEMPX ABTUD LEX

The piece of paper on which you have been working

out the message should now be destroyed to prevent it from falling into enemy hands.

Your contact, who knows that the first four letters of any message he receives form the keyword, uses his cipher wheel to decode the message.

How, here is a message for you to decode. What does it say?

TJOUH FKBBF MDPQO OPWVX VKGHA
CKITS EQARY ATSKU AXGRG BINA

The answer is on page 126.

DOSSIER.. SAH/032
SUBJECT.. Whistle a Tune
CLASSIFICATION.. Secret

This is an advanced form of the alternative sentence code given in dossier SAH/028. Because it is of more practical use to agents on assignment and is not yet known by the enemy it is classified as *secret*. This means that you must take care not to let your list of sentences fall into the hands of unauthorised personnel.

As with the alternative sentence code, you must first make out a list of sentences or instructions that you and your fellow agents are likely to need on a particular assignment. By the side of each sentence write the name of a song that you and your agents know well.

For example:

Follow me to a secret place
Three Blind Mice

Take the next plane out
Greensleeves

Get the plans as soon as possible
Pop Goes The Weasel

Do not come, I'm being watched
Oranges And Lemons

If you want to convey a message to one of your agents you do not even have to approach him or her and risk blowing your cover. All you have to do is whistle the appropriate tune and your agent will get the message. If you are under observation by enemy agents they will not realise that you have passed on a message right under their noses.

A good memory is a useful asset to an agent. If important information is written down it could fall into the wrong hands. Even if the material is in code it can always be deciphered. Therefore whenever possible an agent should rely upon his memory to store important data. This exercise has been devised in order to help you improve your memory. It's called Pelmanism. Agents should team up with another agent to practise it.

Shuffle a pack of playing cards and then spread them out, face down, upon a table. The two agents now take it in turns to flip over any two cards. If the two cards are a pair — two kings, two fours, two aces, and so on — the agent who turned them over removes them from the table and then has another go. If the cards do not match they are simply turned back over face down and left in the same position.

An agent who has a good memory will remember the position of the cards so that when he turns over a card of a similar value to one already turned he can easily form a pair.

When all the cards have been removed from the table, the agent with the highest number of cards is the winner.

Storage
space
for
important
data ...

DOSSIER.. SAH/034
SUBJECT.. Waving the Flag
CLASSIFICATION.. Unrestricted

Semaphore is a method of sending messages using only your hands, or two flags. It was once the principal means of signalling used by the army and the navy.

All secret agents should know and be able to use this system of signalling.

Each letter of the alphabet is signalled by the position of the flags as shown in the chart included in this dossier. It may take a little while to learn the complete alphabet. Learn just a few of the positions each day until you know them all.

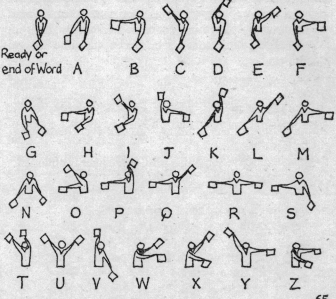

Ready or end of Word   A   B   C   D   E   F

G   H   I   J   K   L   M

N   O   P   Q   R   S

T   U   V   W   X   Y   Z

DOSSIER.. *SAH/035*
SUBJECT.. *Invisible Writing*
CLASSIFICATION.. *Top Secret*

When sending secret messages, all agents are advised to take every precaution to protect classified information. All communications between agents should be in code, but to further protect the data being transmitted it is also a good idea to write important messages in invisible ink.

There are several ways to make invisible writing, some of which involve the use of chemicals. As such items are not generally available to agents in the field the methods described here all use ordinary ingredients. This information is classified *top secret*. Every care must be taken to ensure that these instructions are not revealed to anyone whose credentials have not been checked thoroughly.

Some of the things that can be used as invisible ink are as follows:

Lemon juice. Squeeze the juice out of a lemon and use that instead of ink. Orange juice and grapefruit juice will also be found to be effective.

Milk. Use ordinary milk as your ink and the writing will be invisible.

Onion juice. Grate an onion until some juice is obtained. Use this juice to write your message.

Salt water. Half a teaspoon of ordinary salt dissolved in half a pint of water makes a good invisible ink.

Vinegar. Ordinary vinegar can be used as an invisible ink.

Writing the message. Use an old pen or a sharpened match to write the message.

To make writing visible. If any of these methods are used, the writing can be made visible by the application of heat. Do not heat the paper in front of a fire as the paper may burn and an important message may be lost. Use the heat from a lightbulb, a radiator, or a warm iron to make the writing appear.

IMPORTANT. A sheet of completely blank paper looks very suspicious. If you use invisible ink write the message on every alternate line. On the lines between write another message in ordinary ink. If the paper should go astray the innocent, visible message will be read and no-one will realise that the paper also conveys a secret message written in invisible ink.

DOSSIER.. SAH/036
SUBJECT.. Telephone Scrambler
CLASSIFICATION.. Unrestricted

Try solving this problem designed to test your powers of observation and concentration — essential requirements for every top agent.

The agent in the picture is using only one of the telephones shown at the bottom of the page. Follow the telephone wires to find out which instrument he is using.

DOSSIER.. SAH/037
SUBJECT.. Typewriter Code
CLASSIFICATION.. Secret

This is a development of the code described in dossier SAH/008. For this version you have to be familiar with the layout of the standard typewriter keyboard.

When writing a message, all you have to do is to put down the letter situated to the right of the letter you are coding. Thus the word ATTACK will become SYYSVL.

For practice purposes a message written in this code is given here. Using the typewriter keyboard included in this dossier, can you decipher the message?

JOFRPIY JSD NRRM FODVPBRTRF G:RR
YJR VPIMYTU SY PMVR EO::VPMYSV Y
UPI EJRM YJR VPSDY OD V:RST

The answer can be found on page 126.

69

These drawings were found in the possession of the German secret agent Otto von Coldo. Can you decipher them and read what the message says?

The answer can be found on page 126.

It is often useful for an agent to be aware of the time in different parts of the world. The time calculator described in this dossier will provide an approximate indication of the time in other countries. It should be essential equipment for all Armada agents.

Copy the two dials shown in the blueprint included in this dossier on to a sheet of card and then cut them out. Make a small hole in the centre of each disc and use a paper fastener to pin the two circles of card together. The method of construction is similar to that explained in dossier SAH/029.

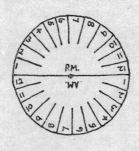

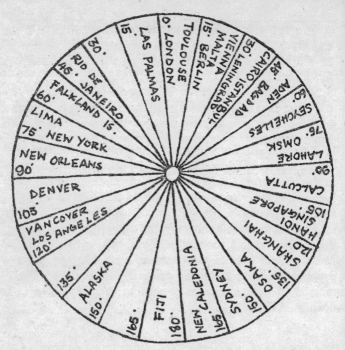

Now, no matter where you are in the world, you can have an indication of what the time is in any other country. This is how the time calculator is used:

Imagine that you are on a secret mission in Singapore and that you have to radio an urgent message to HQ in London. The London operators are, however, off duty from midnight to six o'clock in the morning so there is no point in calling during these times. It is 3 p.m. in Singapore — can you transmit your message? To find out, all you have to do is to turn the inner disc of your time calculator until 3 p.m. is alongside 105° Singapore, Look at 0° and you will see that it is 8 a.m. in London, so you can transmit your message safe in the knowledge that there will be someone on duty to pick it up.

Using your world time calculator, can you answer the following questions?

1. If it is 8 a.m. G.M.T.* in London, what time is it in Calcutta?

2. When it is 4 p.m. in Leningrad, what is the time in New York?

3. It is 7 p.m. in Calcutta. What is the time in Sydney?

4. What time is it in Osaka when it is midnight in Berlin?

5. What time is it in New Orleans when it is 10 a.m. in Buenos Aires?

The answers can be found on page 126.

*The time given on the calculator for London is Greenwich Mean Time. If you use the calculator between Spring and Autumn the time for London should be advanced by one hour.

DOSSIER.. SAH/040
SUBJECT.. Disguise
CLASSIFICATION.. Secret

All agents should master some of the techniques of disguise so that they can meet contacts or carry out assignments without being followed.

It is possible to obtain elaborate disguise outfits but, as the majority of agents have to travel light and fast, it is much more useful to know some of the tricks of the trade that do not require special greasepaints, false beards, or involved make-up.

An agent can disguise himself quite simply with some of the tricks listed here:

Tie a pillow to your stomach with a piece of string to make yourself look fatter.

Wear a pair of sunglasses to hide the upper part of your face.

Wear a pair of spectacles with the lenses removed to change your appearance quite dramatically.

Put pieces of cotton wool in your mouth, between your teeth and your cheeks, to change the shape of your face.

A false moustache can be made quickly and easily with some dark wool and a piece of sticky tape.

Change your hairstyle — part it on the side opposite to normal, or part it in the middle, or comb it straight back.

Change the way you walk. If you normally walk slowly try walking briskly; if you normally walk erect, stoop your shoulders to make yourself look different.

Put a small stone in one of your shoes to give yourself a limp.

Wear a hat to conceal the upper part of your face.

Change your name when signing anything.

Always carry a newspaper or a magazine. It acts as a good place of concealment. You can hide behind it while pretending to be reading.

If you are normally right-handed, become left-handed; if you are normally left-handed, use your right hand for everything.

Change your voice. Speak with a foreign accent or with a broad dialect. If speaking on the telephone put some food in your mouth or cover the mouthpiece with a handkerchief to disguise your voice.

There may well be occasions when you will come into the possession of a message being passed between enemy agents. If this happens, and the message is in code, you will have to break the code to find out what the message says.

One way to do this is to go through the message and count the frequency with which certain letters occur.

If the original message was written in English you can be certain that the letter that appears the highest number of times is E. Count through again and the letter that is used the second highest number of times will probably be a T. Letters used most frequently after this can be seen in the following list which shows the complete alphabet in the order that the letters are most used. The letters that appear together usually occur with about the same frequency.

Some experts will disagree with the exact order of some of the letters but the general trend will still be the same. To test it out for yourself, go through several hundred words of a book and count how many times each of the letters appear (the more words you look at, the more accurate will be your final result). You will find that the frequency of the letters is very close to the list given in this dossier.

To use this information in deciphering a code you carry out a similar test. First go through the coded message and count the number of times that each letter appears. Then, using the frequency table, you will be able to tell what some of the letters are and others you will have to guess at. It is rather like doing a complicated crossword puzzle but with thought and some guesswork you should be able to decode the message eventually. This procedure is explained in more detail in dossier SAH/043.

DOSSIER.. SAH/042
SUBJECT.. Changes at the Frontier
CLASSIFICATION.. ✳✳✳

Imagine that you are approaching a frontier post which you know should look like the first of these two pictures. As you approach the border, you sense that there is something wrong because the post now looks like the second picture. There are in fact ten differences between the two pictures. Can you say what they are?

Answers on page 127.

DOSSIER.. SAH/043
SUBJECT.. Cracking the Code
CLASSIFICATION.. Secret

BZ RS C TSCFFU SDDSJBAHS OLU C YCI
VCO BZ RS SINZPSN PABV C OBTZIG
OLATAB ZD OSFD OCJTADAJS JZHTCGS
CIN OSFD JZIBTZF, PABV BVS LZPST
ZD CJBAIG C LCTB, XMAJW CB
ZROSTHCBAZI CIN NSNMJBAZI, CIN
RFSOOSN PABV GZZN VSCFBV CIN
ISTHS ZD SKJSLBAZICF XMCFABU

If you captured an enemy spy with that message in his
pocket, would you know what it said? An agent should
have an idea of how to crack codes like this. In the
majority of cases all he will have to do is to transmit the
message to the computer centre at headquarters but
there may be times when this is not possible. The instructions given in this dossier will enable agents in the
field to decipher most messages by themselves.

First you will need to know the frequency with which
letters are likely to appear in such a message. This
information will be found in dossier SAH/041.

The first step in cracking the code is to count how
many times each letter appears in the message. If you
count the letters in the message at the head of this dossier,
you will find that they occur as follows:

S = 23 times	T = 10 times	R = 4
C = 20	F = 9	H = 4
B = 18	J = 9	M = 4
Z = 17	D = 8	U = 3
A = 14	V = 7	X = 2
I = 13	P = 5	K = 1
N = 10	L = 5	W = 1
O = 10	G = 4 times	Y = 1

If we compare just the first four letters with the normal frequency table it is easy to guess that S must equal *e*, C will be *t*, B is *a* or *o*, and Z is *a* or *o*.

But if you look a little closer you will see that the letter C in the coded message stands alone on occasion so it cannot represent the letter *t* but must be the letter *a*. This means that we can no deduce that:

$$S = e$$
$$C = a$$

B is probably *t*

Z is probably *o*

If we try substituting these letters into the message we get this result:

TO - E A - EA - - - E - - E - T - - EA - A - - A -
TO - E E - - O - E - - - T - A - T - O - - - - - - - T
O - - E - F - A - - - - - - E - O - - A - EA - - - E - -
- O - T - O - - - T - T - E - O - E - O - A - T - - -
A - A - T - - - - - AT O - - E - - AT - O - A - -
- E - - - T - O - A - - - - E - - E - - T - - OO -
- EA - T - A - - - E - - E O - E - - E - T - O - A -
- - A - - T -

Now let us try some deduction. In the coded message there are three two-letter words ZD. We know that Z=*o* so the complete word must be OR, ON, or OF. Therefore D in the coded message must represent R, N, or F. If you look at the normal frequency table and compare it with the frequency table drawn up for the code message, you will see that F is the nearest of these three letters to the position of the letter D in the code frequency table. From this you can assume that it is quite likely that D=f.

In the message there is a three-letter word BVS. We know that B=t and that S=e so it is quite likely that the middle letter is h. In this case the position of V and h in the two frequency tables are not that close but they are near enough for us to try substituting the letter h for V throughout the message.

There are also four words coded as CIN. As we know that they begin with a, we can guess that the word is "and". If this is the case I=n, and N=d.

If we put in all the letters that we now think we know, we can see that the message is already beginning to fill up. This is the stage that we have reached:

```
TO - E A - EA - - - EFFE - T - - E - - - A - AN
HA - TO - E ENDO - ED - - TH A - T - ON -
- - - - - T OF - E - F - A - - - F - - E - O - - A - E
AND - E - F - ONTO - O - - - TH THE - O - E
OF A - T - N - A - A - T - - - - - AT O - - E - - A -
T - ON AND DED - - T - ON AND - - E - - ED
- - TH - O O D HEA - TH AND NE - - E OF
E - - E - T - ONA - - - A - - T -
```

Carrying on in the same fashion look at the two-letter words RS. Because the S=e, and because the word in both the places that it occurs is preceded by the word "to", we can assume that the word itself is "be" and that R=b.

Going back to the code frequency table in this dossier we find that we have now covered the first seven letters with the exception of A. If we compare this table with the frequency table given in dossier SAH/041 we can deduce that A probably represents the letter i.

Looking again at the coded message we find that there

are two words coded as PABV. As we know that A, B, and V are *i*, *t*, and *h*, we can guess that the complete word is "with" and that P=*w*.

Put all these new letters in our blank version of the message and you will see that we are well on the way to completing the whole thing:

TO BE A –EA––– EFFE–TI–E ––– A –AN
HA– TO BE ENDOWED WITH A –T–ON–
––I–IT OF –E–F –A––IFI–E –O––A–E
AND –E–F –ONT–O– WITH THE –OWE–
OF A–TIN– A –A–T ––I–– AT OB–E–A–
––TION AND DED––TION AND B–E––ED
WITH –OOD HEA–TH AND NE––E OF
E––E–TIONA– ––A–IT–

See if you can now carry on and complete the message. Here are some clues to help you:

Look at the eighth word, – AN. What can that be? (*Ban, can, dan, fan, man, pan, ran, tan,* or *van?*)

And is the ninth word *had, has, hag, ham, hat,* or *hay*?

What is the most likely final letter for the twenty-eighth word, A – TIN – ?

And what about the thirty-ninth word? Is it *food, good, hood, mood,* or *wood*?

Guess at some of the other words and try substituting the letters you find and see what effect this has on the rest of the message.

A final clue: The whole message is how Lord Baden Powell once described the qualities required of a good spy or secret agent. The complete decoded message can be found on page 127.

Now try this method of decoding with messages compiled by a fellow agent and see if you can work out what they say.

DOSSIER.. SAH/044
SUBJECT.. It's in the Stars
CLASSIFICATION.. Unrestricted

All agents should know how they can tell in which direction they are travelling by looking at the stars.

If you are north of the equator all you have to do is look for the north star, Polaris. Face towards it and you are facing north. To find Polaris look for the Plough, a group of six stars in the Great Bear (Ursa Major) constellation, and follow the direction of the two stars at the end of this group. A short distance away you will see another star all by itself. This is Polaris.

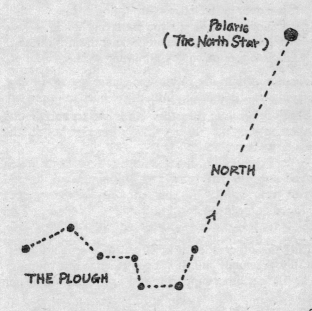

If you are south of the equator Polaris will not be visible. In this case you look for the Southern Cross, a prominent constellation formed by four bright stars. The long arm of the cross points towards the south.

The stars of the Southern Cross.

SOUTH

Another way to tell in which direction you are facing is to get a straight stick and point it at any bright star. Look along the stick, as if looking along the barrel of a rifle, and watch the star closely. In a minute or so you will see the star move.

If it moves to the left you are facing north.
If it moves to the right you are facing south.
If it moves upwards you are looking towards the east.
And if it goes down you are facing west.

These directions are easy to remember if you visualise the points of the compass turned one quarter to the left as shown here.

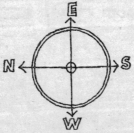

During this observation it is, of course, essential to keep the stick absolutely still. It is a good idea to rest your arm on a wall or another support to make sure that you do not move.

84

Your mission, should you choose to accept it, is to photograph a list of agents working for SAWD (Sabotage And Worldwide Destruction). This list is concealed in the document room at SAWD HQ in Nevistan, Outer Mongolia, but the room is cunningly concealed by a labrynth of passages. Our agent on the inside will get you into the Administration Area near the main entrance, but can you find a way through the maze to the document room?

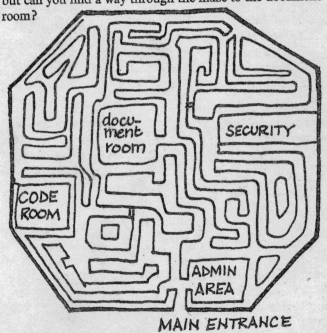

DOSSIER.. SAH/046
SUBJECT.. Groundwork
CLASSIFICATION.. ✳✳✳

If you have to leave a signal for someone in open country, use the codes shown in this dossier. They will only mean something to other Armada agents.

Go this way

Return to H.Q

Meet here tonight

Get out of the country

mission abandoned.

Stay here

This is a useful means of sending short messages to other agents.

Write a letter to someone. This letter does not convey your secret message but is merely a decoy to put enemy agents off the scent should they intercept and open your colleague's mail. The letter is placed inside the envelope and the envelope addressed in the normal way.

Now you write your secret message — on the envelope! It is written in very small letters on the top right-hand corner of the envelope. The smaller the letters, the longer the message can be. The whole message is then covered with the postage stamp. If the message is long use more than one stamp.

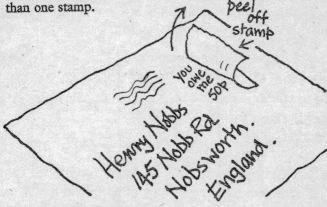

When your fellow agent receives the letter he does not bother to open it but simply steams off the stamp to read what you have written.

DOSSIER.. SAH/048
SUBJECT.. Domino Code
CLASSIFICATION.. Top Secret

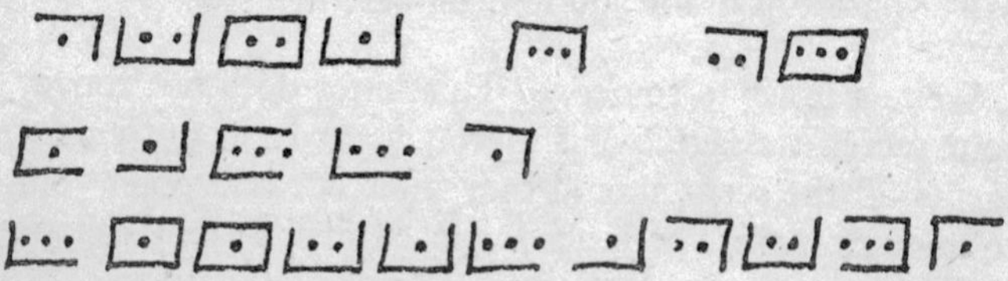

Can you read this message? What it says is: "Send X to Paris immediately." The code that has been used is called the domino code because the figures look like dominoes. Some agents will know it by its other name, "the Rosicrucian code". This is how it works:

First draw a grid as shown below, and in each square place three letters of the alphabet, like this:

ABC	DEF	GHI
JKL	MNO	PQR
STU	VWX	YZ

In writing a message each letter of the alphabet is indicated by the type of box in which it is enclosed and one, two, or three dots within the box to identify the particular letter being coded. Thus A is coded as ⬜, C is ⬜ , and W is ⬜

Here is a message for you to decipher:

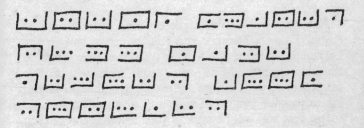

The answer can be found on page 127.

DOSSIER.. SAH/049
SUBJECT.. Field Telephone
CLASSIFICATION.. Unrestricted

This field telephone will be found invaluable to an agent who wishes to communicate with another agent during an operation.

All you need are two clean tin cans and a length of string. Using a hammer and nail, punch a hole in the bottom of each of the tins so that the string can be threaded through. Mind your fingers when you do this for agents of your calibre are extremely valuable. If you injure yourself you could weaken your group to such an extent that you will be putting your fellow agents at risk.

Having threaded the string through the holes, tie a number of knots in each end of the string so that it will not fall out of the cans.

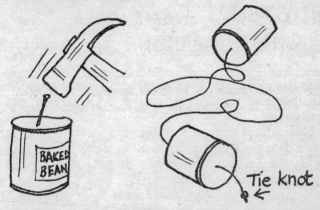

If the string is held taut between the two tin cans, you can speak into one of the tins and your fellow agent will be able to receive your message at the other end of the line.

DOSSIER.. SAH/050
SUBJECT.. Watermarks
CLASSIFICATION.. Top Secret

This is a useful way of sending secret messages when the invisible inks detailed in dossier SAH/035 are not available.

Take a sheet of paper and soak it in water. Now lay it down on top of a mirror or a sheet of glass. Place a sheet of dry paper on top of this and write your message with a pencil or a ball-point pen.

Remove the top sheet and destroy it. When the wet sheet has dried, it can be passed to other agents quite openly because it looks just like a sheet of ordinary paper.

To make the message visible, all you have to do is to soak the paper in water once more and the message appears on the paper like a watermark. As soon as the paper dries, the writing will become invisible once more.

It is as well to disguise the piece of paper since a blank sheet may arouse suspicion. One way to disguise it is to write a visible message on the top half and the invisible message on the lower half.

Another way to disguise the paper is to make it into the shape of an envelope and put an ordinary letter inside it. No-one will think that the important part of the letter is in fact the envelope.

Good observation is absolutely vital to a secret agent. To become a top agent it is necessary to develop your powers of observation to a high degree. One way to do this is to practise tests like the one given in this dossier.

Look at the first picture for three minutes and try to remember all the objects shown.

In the picture over the page the objects have been moved around and five items have been left out altogether. Without looking back at the first picture, can you name the five objects that are missing?

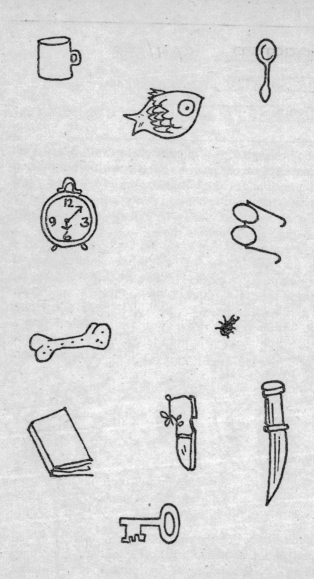

In 1837, Samuel Morse, in collaboration with Alfred Vail, devised a system of signals for the telegraphic transmission of information. The code was revised in 1844 and again in 1851 when an international conference combined four similar systems into the system we now know as "Morse code".

Morse code is still used today for both civil and military purposes and should therefore form part of the armoury of every agent. It is particularly useful because it can be transmitted in many different ways. It can be tapped out on a simple tin can, or on complicated telegraphic apparatus; it can be written; it can be flashed with a torch, or transmitted by a heliograph. It can even be transmitted in one of the codes described in this handbook.

It can be flashed with a torch ...

Like the semaphore code described in dossier SAH/034, morse should be learned bit by bit until the whole code is known. In the code a dot represents a short signal and a dash a long signal.

A	· —		O	— — —
B	— · · ·		P	· — — ·
C	— · — ·		Q	— — · —
D	— · ·		R	· — ·
E	·		S	· · ·
F	· · — ·		T	—
G	— — ·		U	· · —
H	· · · ·		V	· · · —
I	· ·		W	· — —
J	· — — —		X	— · · —
K	— · —		Y	— · — —
L	· — · ·		Z	— — · ·
M	— —		full stop	· — · — · —
N	— ·		question mark	· · — — · ·

There may be times, whilst on assignment, that an agent has to sleep out in the countryside. This could be due to the fact that he is being pursued by enemy agents or because it is not safe for him to be seen in populated areas. There may also be occasions when an agent has to wait in a remote spot to be picked up or to meet other agents. At such times it is useful to know how to construct makeshift living quarters.

Simple shelters can easily be made as follows:

1. Find five or six long sticks and tie them together at one end with your belt, a piece of string, vines, or anything else that is handy for the purpose. Place the sticks on the ground so that they form a pyramid. Cover this framework with an old blanket or pieces of sacking, and then cover that with grass. The grass helps to camouflage the shelter and also ensures that it is nice and warm inside.

Tie the sticks together at one end with your belt...

2. A simple tent can be made with a length of string and a blanket quite easily. Tie the string between two trees and then simply throw the blanket over it and weigh the edges down with some large stones.

3. If the string you have is not long enough to be tied from tree to tree as in method two, then make your tent this way:

Tie one end of the string round a tree or to one of its branches and the other end to a stick. Peg the stick into the ground and then throw the blanket over the string, weighing the edges down with stones as before.

DOSSIER.. SAH /054

SUBJECT.. The Vigenère Tableau

CLASSIFICATION.. Top Secret

In 1587, Blaise de Vigenère, a Frenchman, published a book called *A Treatise on Secret Writing*. In the book he described an ingenious coding method now known as the Vigenère Tableau. It is a method that should be known and adopted by all agents.

The table devised by Vigenère looks like this:

```
A A B C D E F G H I J K L M N O P Q R S T U V W X Y Z
A a b c d e f g h i j k l m n o p q r s t u v w x y z
B b c d e f g h i j k l m n o p q r s t u v w x y z a
C c d e f g h i j k l m n o p q r s t u v w x y z a b
D d e f g h i j k l m n o p q r s t u v w x y z a b c
E e f g h i j k l m n o p q r s t u v w x y z a b c d
F f g h i j k l m n o p q r s t u v w x y z a b c d e
G g h i j k l m n o p q r s t u v w x y z a b c d e f
H h i j k l m n o p q r s t u v w x y z a b c d e f g
I i j k l m n o p q r s t u v w x y z a b c d e f g h
J j k l m n o p q r s t u v w x y z a b c d e f g h i
K k l m n o p q r s t u v w x y z a b c d e f g h i j
L l m n o p q r s t u v w x y z a b c d e f g h i j k
M m n o p q r s t u v w x y z a b c d e f g h i j k l
N n o p q r s t u v w x y z a b c d e f g h i j k l m
O o p q r s t u v w x y z a b c d e f g h i j k l m n
P p q r s t u v w x y z a b c d e f g h i j k l m n o
Q q r s t u v w x y z a b c d e f g h i j k l m n o p
R r s t u v w x y z a b c d e f g h i j k l m n o p q
S s t u v w x y z a b c d e f g h i j k l m n o p q r
T t u v w x y z a b c d e f g h i j k l m n o p q r s
U u v w x y z a b c d e f g h i j k l m n o p q r s t
V v w x y z a b c d e f g h i j k l m n o p q r s t u
W w x y z a b c d e f g h i j k l m n o p q r s t u v
X x y z a b c d e f g h i j k l m n o p q r s t u v w
Y y z a b c d e f g h i j k l m n o p q r s t u v w x
Z z a b c d e f g h i j k l m n o p q r s t u v w x y
```

At first sight it may look rather complicated but if you look a little closer you will find that it is not necessary to spend hours memorising it, for it is all in alphabetical order with the first letter repeated in each case.

This is how the table is used:

Let us assume that you wish to code the message THE COAST IS CLEAR.

First you and your contact must decide upon a keyword. This can be any word that you like but it should be changed from time to time so that the enemy do not have a chance to discover it.

For this example we will use the codeword UNDERCOVER.

Write out the message and write the codeword, repeated the necessary number of times, over the top like this:

UND ERCOV ER UNDER
THE COAST IS CLEAR

Now take the first letter (T) of the message and run along the top of the table until you reach that letter. Then go down the table until you are level with the first letter (U) of the codeword. The letter at the point where the two lines meet is the letter you use for the first letter of the code message. In this case it is N. Do the same with the second letters of the message and the codeword and you get U. Continue like this throughout the message, and THE COAST IS CLEAR becomes NUH GFCGO MJ WYHEI.

When your colleague receives the message he reverses the process to find out what it says.

First he writes the message down with the keyword over the top, like this:

UND ERCOV ER UNDER
NUH GFCGO MJ WYHEI

The he does almost the same as you did. He takes the

first letter of the codeword (U) and runs down that column until he reaches the first letter of message (N), then he goes across the line to find the first letter of the original message was T. He continues like this until he has deciphered the complete message.

Now, using the Vigenère Tableau, can you put the first of these two messages into code and can you decipher the second message? The keyword in each case is FIREFLY.

1. Enemy tanks sighted.

2. DWLV RTQXQFR ND RT QEJNWRWIKI
   JYCRG YIFOOZIIXJCQ

Turn to page 127 to see if you have got them right.

DOSSIER.. SAH/055
SUBJECT.. More Burglar Alarms
CLASSIFICATION.. Unrestricted

A few old tin cans or some strips of metal will form an effective burglar alarm for your headquarters. Tie the tins to a length of string. The easiest way to do this is to punch holes in the base of each tin as shown in dossier SAH/049. Now pin the other end of the string to the wall or the ceiling of your HQ, just behind the door, so that when the door is opened it will hit the tins and sound off the alarm.

Another way to set up this type of alarm is to have a length of wool, or weak cotton, running across the entrance to your HQ. One end of the cotton is tied to a post and the cotton is then run across the entrance and over the branch of a tree, or a hook in another post, on the other side of the entrance. The tins are tied to this end of the cotton.

When someone walks towards your HQ they will break the cotton and the tins will fall to the ground, warning you that someone is coming.

DOSSIER.. SAH/056
SUBJECT.. Candle Hideaway
CLASSIFICATION.. ✳✳✳

This is a useful way to hide secret documents in your headquarters.

Get a sheet of white card and make it into a tube. Now push a piece of candle into the top of the tube and a piece into the bottom. Use the rest of the candle to rub down the sides of the tube so that it looks like a real candle which can now be placed in a candle holder on your desk.

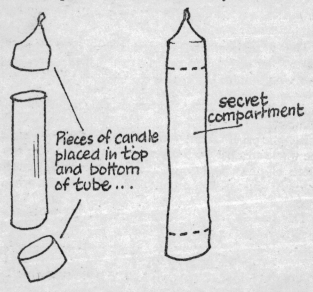

Pieces of candle placed in top and bottom of tube...

secret compartment

It look just like an ordinary and innocent candle and no-one will realise that secret documents are hidden within its hollow centre.

DOSSIER.. SAH/057
SUBJECT.. Document Copier
CLASSIFICATION.. ✳✳✳

Although miniature cameras are standard equipment for all agents, there may be times when you have to copy a secret document and there is not enough light to photograph it or you do not have your camera with you. The secret formula given in this dossier will enable you to copy documents without a camera.

Get an old saucer and place in it one teaspoonful of turpentine, one teaspoonful of washing-up liquid, and two teaspoonfuls of water.

To copy a picture or written information, follow these instructions:

With a sponge or a piece of old cloth, dab some of the formula on to the information to be copied.

Now place a sheet of white paper on top of the document.

Rub the paper carefully with the back of a spoon until the whole area has been covered. Now separate the two sheets of paper and there should be a perfect, though reversed, copy of the original document on the white sheet.

This process works best when the original document is on newsprint or something similar

> **REMEMBER !**
> THIS FORMULA IS CLASSIFIED INFORMATION
> DO NOT PASS
> THIS INFORMATION ON TO ANYONE.

DOSSIER.. SAH/058
SUBJECT.. Hard Boiled Eggs
CLASSIFICATION.. Top Secret

This method of sending secret messages was used by German agents during both the First and the Second World War.

If you have to interrogate a simple peasant woman who has with her only a basket of fruit and eggs, you will probably let her go without question. But you could be making a deadly mistake, for those eggs in her basket are not so innocent as they appear. They are her means of carrying information about troop movements to the enemy.

If you were to pick up one of the eggs and break off the shell, you would find secret information written on the *inside* of the egg!

This is how the information gets inside the egg: Mix some alum (available from the chemist) with vinegar and use this ink to write upon the shell of the egg. A matchstick is the best thing to use as a pen. As the ink dries the message will disappear.

The next thing to do is to boil the egg. This causes the message to go through the shell and on to the white of the egg. So the egg appears to be perfectly ordinary — until you remove the shell when the writing is revealed.

Eggs like this can be left in your headquarters as a way of leaving messages to other agents who may go into the building when you are out.

DOSSIER.. SAH/059
SUBJECT.. Silent Signals
CLASSIFICATION.. ✳✳✳

There will be times during a mission that you will have to make contact with another agent knowing that one of you is under the surveillance of an enemy agent. In such emergencies it is useful to know a silent code so that you can warn your colleague without anyone knowing that you have made contact.

The signals used in a silent code should appear to be perfectly natural actions. The signals shown in this dossier have been designed with this in mind. They will not be noticed by the enemy and you and your colleagues can communicate in confidence.

"He knows who you are"

scratch scratch

"I won't be here long"

"I'll see you tomorrow" →

Now invent some of your own signals to add to the code.

Morse code, which is described in dossier SAH/052 can be transmitted in many different forms. This agent flying a kite appears to be engaged in an innocent pastime — but look at the tail of the kite. If the bows represent dashes and the knots are dots, what is the message that the agent is transmitting to his contact?

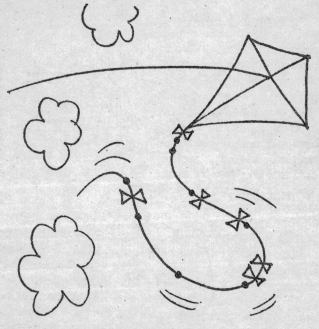

The answer can be found on page 127.

DOSSIER.. SAH/061
SUBJECT.. Through the Holes
CLASSIFICATION.. ✳✳✳

Here is a simple method of sending secret messages that does not involve a code. If the message should get intercepted by an enemy agent, he will find it very difficult, if not impossible, to decipher without the special device that does all the work for you.

To make this device you will need a sheet of card or paper. Cut several holes in the card so that it looks something like the one in the blueprint included in this dossier. When you have done this, lay it on top of another sheet of card and use the first as a template to make another card that is exactly the same. You have one card and your contact has the other.

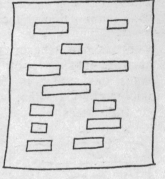

This is how you use the card to write a secret message.

Place the card on a sheet of paper and write the message through the holes, placing one word in each space. Your message will now look like the second illustration.

All you have to do now is to write lots of meaningless words around your message so that the paper appears to be a jumbled mass of nonsense as in the third illustration. It is now impossible to read the original message.

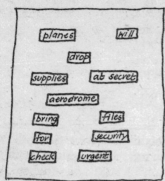

drop parachutes by fifteen will planes make a will. for allow them window ring a make and drop submarine grass food is reports obvious do supplies need at secret and we runway ships come urgent for its aerodrome papers can house secret telephone film a not bring parcel to files come need write police guns allow and for urgent a security call can telephone arrange papers to check meet urgent secret men concern planes meeting.

When your contact receives the message he simply places his card on top of the sheet of paper and reads the words showing through the holes. It is as simple as that!

WARNING: THE SECRECY AND EFFECTIVENESS OF THIS METHOD DEPENDS UPON AGENTS GUARDING THEIR CARDS CAREFULLY. DO NOT LET AN ENEMY AGENT DISCOVER YOUR CARD. KEEP IT IN A SAFE PLACE AT ALL TIMES.

DOSSIER.. SAH/062
SUBJECT.. Picture Post
CLASSIFICATION.. Unrestricted

The postcards shown in this dossier were found in the hotel room of Anatole Clavinsky, top agent for GHOST (Global Havoc Our Secret Task). They had been sent to him from his informants in other parts of the world. Can you tell from the pictures on the postcards the countries from which Clavinsky's informants operate?

The answers can be found on page 127.

This list of times is not as straightforward as it seems. Can you work out what they represent and then read the message that is hidden in them?

quarter past eight	twenty past eight
five past eleven	five to twelve
twenty past nine	quarter past three
eleven o'clock	quarter past eleven
five past eight	quarter to four
five past six	five past six
twenty to six	twenty to four
four o'clock	six o'clock
half past one	quarter to eight
five to six	half past one
quarter to eleven	twenty to one
five to one	nine o'clock

If you are completely baffled here's a clue; try drawing the times on clock faces.

If you are still baffled you will find the answer on page 127.

IMPORTANT: If you use this method to send messages, do not just write out a list of times, but make the page look like a list of train times, or a railway timetable.

DOSSIER.. SAH/064
SUBJECT.. *Reading the Lawn*
CLASSIFICATION.. *Secret*

The picture in this file looks innocent. But it contains a secret message. If you look closely at the blades of grass you will find that some are long and some are short. Could they represent morse code? If they do represent morse, and each flower represents the end of a word, what does the message say?

You will find the answer on page 127.

DOSSIER.. SAH/065
SUBJECT.. Crosswords
CLASSIFICATION.. ✳✳✳

This method of sending secret messages is foolproof. Guard the secret carefully. It is very easy to do but impossible to decode if you do not know the method.

First you must draw up a crossword grid, something like the one shown in this dossier. It does not have to be the same as the one shown here. In fact, for obvious reasons of security it must not be the same as this example. Your contact must also have a copy of your crossword layout.

Now write your message in the blank squares of the crossword, starting from the top and entering it along the first line, then across the second line, and so on.

This drawing shows how the messages "*Meet aeroplane at dawn and pick up new agent for special mission. All agents in area have been notified*" is written on the grid.

When the message is on the crossword grid it is then transferred to another sheet of paper, but the letters are taken from the grid from top to bottom so the message sent to your contact will read:

LCGSE MAWKESIEE ENUPONENI
ENANENAE ENTCTHD TAPIASANX
ATNFALIOP EDEOLLNTR RDPRMAVO
OAIWIGAEI PASRBF

This, of course, means absolutely nothing to anyone except your fellow agent who has a copy of the crossword grid. As soon as he receives the message he writes it downwards on the blank squares of the crossword and is able to see what you wrote originally.

Because, in this instance, the message was too short to fill the grid completely, the meaningless letters X, P, R, and O, were put in to fill the empty squares.

Using the same grid, can you understand this message

SEARR BSPTSEDEE OOODSNTHI
RISPAHHO NSLSWAR DGNTAATEN
ENIAHVRRZ RIGNEENER COBNGBWQ
RTLHUEEEP OTADAZ

The answer is on page 127.

DOSSIER.. SAH/066
SUBJECT.. Book Safe
CLASSIFICATION.. ✳✳✳

A useful hiding place for secret codes, foreign currency,
and other items which will never be discovered by enemy
agents can be made as follows:

Get an old telephone directory, the thicker it is the
better, and open it about one third of the way from the
front page. Now cut a large hole in the centre of every
page from that position all the way to the back of the
book. Be careful that you do not cut yourself when doing
this. Good agents are hard to find and an injured agent
means the loss of valuable manpower.

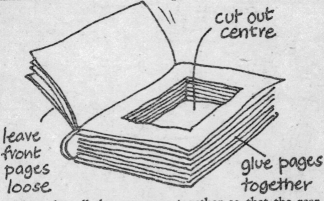

cut out
centre

leave
front
pages
loose

glue pages
together

Next glue all the cut pages together so that the rear
portion of the book forms a small box in which top
security items can be hidden. When the book is placed
alongside with ordinary telephone directories, it will take
an extremely talented counter spy to detect such an
unusual hiding place.

119

An alternative method of construction is to cut only the centre pages of the book and glue these together so that the pages at the front and back of the book are unrestricted and the book appears innocent to the casual observer.

Either version makes a valuable hiding place for secret items and yet it looks just like an ordinary telephone book.

DOSSIER.. SAH/067
SUBJECT.. Handy Timepiece
CLASSIFICATION.. Secret

There may be occasions when you are on assignment in enemy territory and you do not have with you any way of telling the time. If you ask one of the locals you may be in danger of blowing your cover. The instructions in the dossier enable you to know the time even though you are not wearing a watch.

Find a straight stick about ten centimetres in length and hold it between your thumb and forefinger. Now hold your hand up to face the sun and move it into a position that causes the shadow of the ball of your thumb to just touch the line of life. The line of life is what fortune tellers call the line that runs from the centre of your wrist and around the base of the thumb to about halfway between the thumb and forefinger.

When the shadow is positioned correctly the shadow cast by the stick will tell you the hour of the day in accordance with the numbers shown on the blueprint included in this dossier.

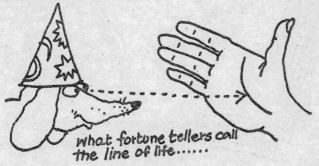

what fortune tellers call
the line of life......

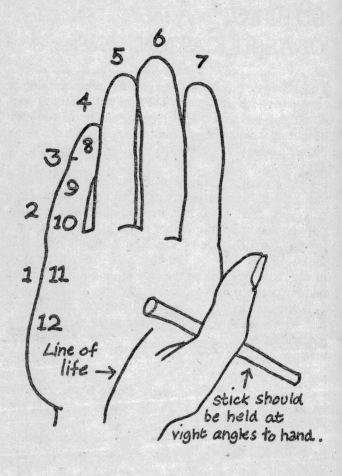

5 6 7
4
3 8
9
2 10
1 11
12
Line of
life →

stick should
be held at
right angles to hand.

DOSSIER.. SAH/068
SUBJECT.. Agents' Proficiency Test
CLASSIFICATION.. Top Secret

To test whether or not a new agent has reached a degree of efficiency that will make him a valuable asset to your group, give him this test. If he passes, he will have the qualities required of a top agent:

1. The agent must be able to trail another agent for a distance of at least half a mile without the other person being aware that he is being followed.

2. He should complete an assault course (see SAH/022) within the time stipulated.

3. He should be able to decode a message given to him by another agent.

4. He must do a good deed for someone without letting them know who did it.

5. He should be able to hide a secret message on himself where no-one can find it.

6. He must be able to disguise himself so that someone who knows him does not recognise him.

7. His reflexes must be quick. Test him with the reaction tester described in dossier SAH/003.

8. Blindfold him and then lead him to a place nearby. He must tell you where he is without removing the blindfold.

9. He should be sent on a not-too-dangerous mission in enemy territory and return to base without being harmed.

10. Have another agent trail him. He must try to get away from the person who is following.

When he can do all the things set out in the test he can be admitted as a full member of your group. He will make a fine secret agent and may now be permitted to read the dossiers contained in this handbook.

An agent must be able to disguise himself so that someone who knows him does not recognise him.

002 Birmingham; Cairo; Moscow; Peking; Rome; Venice.

012 The complete shopping list reads: ABANDON
MISSION.

016 Canoe hidden near waterfall as arranged.

020 They are the numbers one to seven, each with
its reversed image. The missing number is six.

025 Beware soldiers are searching your area.
Three submarines reported in your area. Find out their
exact position and report back.

027 MI6 — The British Special Intelligence Service concerned with espionage and intelligence abroad.

CIA — Central Intelligence Agency. American Secret
Service concerned with espionage and intelligence
abroad.

GRU — Glavnoye Razvedyvatenoye Upravleniye
(Chief Intelligence Administration). Russian Military
Intelligence.

MI5 — British Security Service concerned with internal
security.

FBI — Federal Bureau of Investigation. American
Security Service concerned with internal security and
counter espionage.

KGB — Komitent Gosudarstvenoi Bezopasnosti (Com-
mittee for State Security). Chief Russian Intelligence
Service.

031 Meet secret agent XYZ in the market square at midnight.

036 The agent is using telephone number 2.

037 Hideout has been discovered. Flee the country at once.
Will contact you when the coast is clear.

038 Meet me in the old lighthouse at four o'clock to discuss
how we can steal the plans for the new submarine.

039 1. 2pm; 2. 9am; 3. 11pm; 4. 8am; 5. 8am.

042 In the second picture the bird has three whiskers on the
right side of its head; there are only two lines round the

door of the sentry-hut; the sentry's gun is longer; he has three stripes on his left arm; there is no button on his right epaulette; there is no button on his right pocket; there is an extra stake in the fence on the left; there is an extra nail in the fence on the right; there are only two eyelets in his left boot; the sole of his right boot is thicker.

043 To be a really effective spy a man has to be endowed with a strong spirit of self sacrifice courage and self control, with the power of acting a part, quick at observation and deduction, and blessed with good health and nerve of exceptional quality.

045 Did you reach the document room?

048 Enemy planes will make secret drop tonight.

054 1. JVVQD EYSSJ WNRFYMU.

2. Your mission is to infiltrate enemy headquarters.

060 Danger.

062 1. France (Eiffel tower — Paris); 2. Australia (Opera House — Sydney); 3. Italy (Leaning tower — Pisa); 4. U.S.A. (Statue of Liberty — New York); 5. England (Tower bridge — London); 6. Greece (Acropolis — Athens).

063 The times should be seen as if they were on a clock face, and the clock hands represent the arm positions in semaphore. (Note that every semaphore position can be shown by two different times. The letter R, for instance, in which both arms are stretched out straight, could be either a quarter to three or a quarter past nine.)

The coded message reads: Must leave country. Send help.

064 I have plans for new missile. Contact me urgently.

067 Border crossing not possible tonight as planned as the guards have been warned that we are here. PZIORNZRQ (last nine letters used purely to fill the empty squares).

has a whole shipload
of exciting books for you

Armadas are chosen by children all over the world. They're designed to fit your pocket, and your pocket money too. They're colourful, exciting, and there are hundreds of titles to choose from. Armada has something for everyone:

Mystery and adventure series to collect, with favourite characters and authors . . . like Alfred Hitchcock and The Three Investigators – the Hardy Boys – young detective Nancy Drew – the intrepid Lone Piners – Biggles – the rascally William – and others.

Hair-raising Spinechillers – Ghost, Monster and Science Fiction stories. Fascinating quiz and puzzle books. Exciting hobby books. Lots of hilarious fun books. Many famous stories. Thrilling pony adventures. Popular school stories – and many more.

You can build up your own Armada collection – and new Armadas are published every month, so look out for the latest additions to the Captain's cargo.

Armadas are available in bookshops and newsagents

Armada